Empowerment is balance
balance is authenticity
authenticity is Empowerment

LAYDA b

dP

Authenticism

The Layda b catalogue

Christine Layda is the founder and owner of the brand LAYDA b & Authenticist™.

Editing team: Joana Branco, Sofia Castela

ISBN 979-8-218-78265-8
eBook ISBN 979-8-218-78266-5

laydabshoe

This catalogue is designed to be seen by anyone in the Western world. @laydabshoe supports indigenous cultures and minorities.

laydabshoe

Authenticism
#involutionary #thelaydab

laydabshoe

Individual additions are always in style.
#onemodelconcept #thelaydab

laydabshoe

Goes along with true individuality.
#busyLiving #thelaydab

laydabshoe

Albert Einstein said
#symmetry #thelaydab

Everything should be made
as simple as possible, but not simpler.

laydabshoe

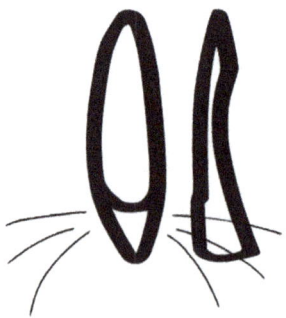

Catwalk is on velvet paws.
#aestheticsandease #thelaydab

laydabshoe

Find the way back, to go forward.
#timeless #thelaydab

laydabshoe

Equal importance of the feminine and masculine,
instead of being equal, matters.
#intertwined #thelaydab

Class is a way of being
La classe è un modo di essere
La classe est une façon d'être
Classe é um jeito de ser
La clase es una forma de ser
Klasse ist eine Art zu sein
気 品 こ そ 生 き 方 で あ る 。

Got to be Real
#dP #thelaydab

laydabshoe

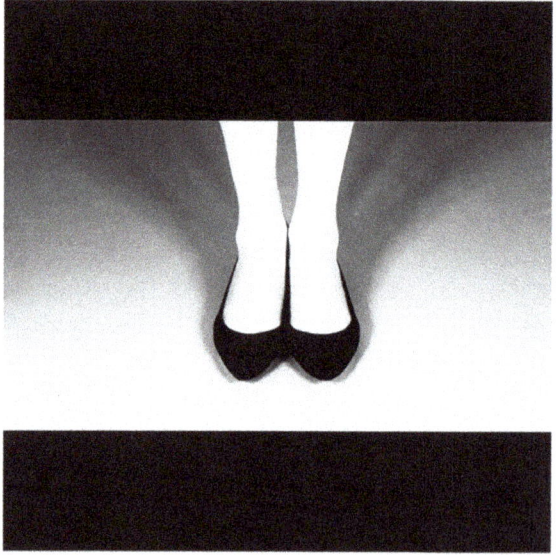

Directions
#nomatterwhat #thelaydab

laydabshoe

This Is It
#uturn #thelaydab

laydabshoe

LAYDA b

be bold
#bauthenticist #thelaydab

laydabshoe

The history of civilization could actually be written in terms of the level of its women.

Fulton J. Sheen

#balancingup #thelaydab

laydabshoe

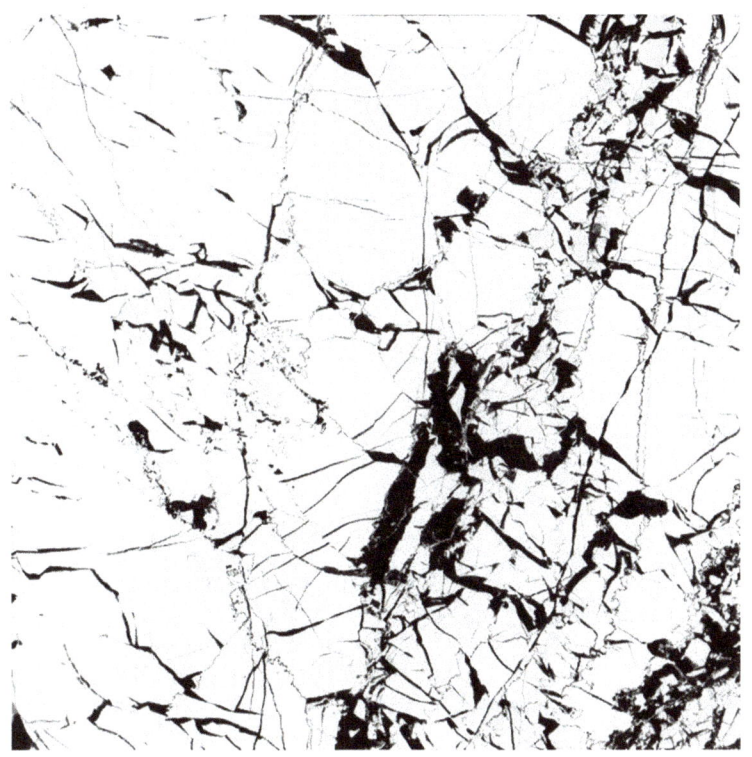

Introfaction
#focused #thelaydab

laydabshoe

You and I must make a pact, we must bring salvation back...
Michael Jackson
#consciousdesign #thelaydab

laydabshoe

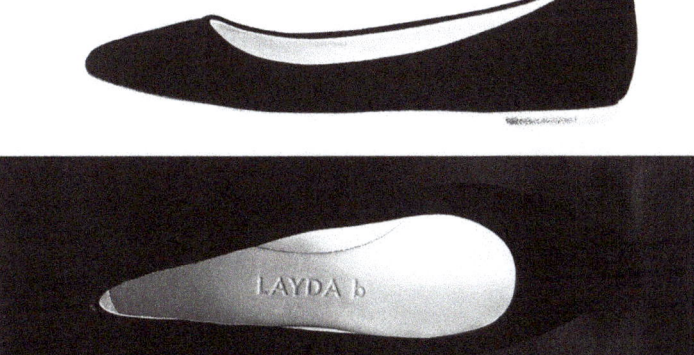

BlackorWhite
#moonwalker #thelaydab

laydabshoe

Hailku Mountain tops
Mountains' buoyant tops, swallows around #unerring
Not bound but bouncy
#hashtaghaiku #thelaydab

laydabshoe

laydabshoe

LAYDA b

What is your Lado B?
#brightside #thelaydab

laydabshoe

Straight-up
#feetintheclouds #thelaydab

laydabshoe

Manekin
#authenticism #thelaydab

laydabshoe

laydabshoe

Crosswalk
#action #thelaydab

laydabshoe

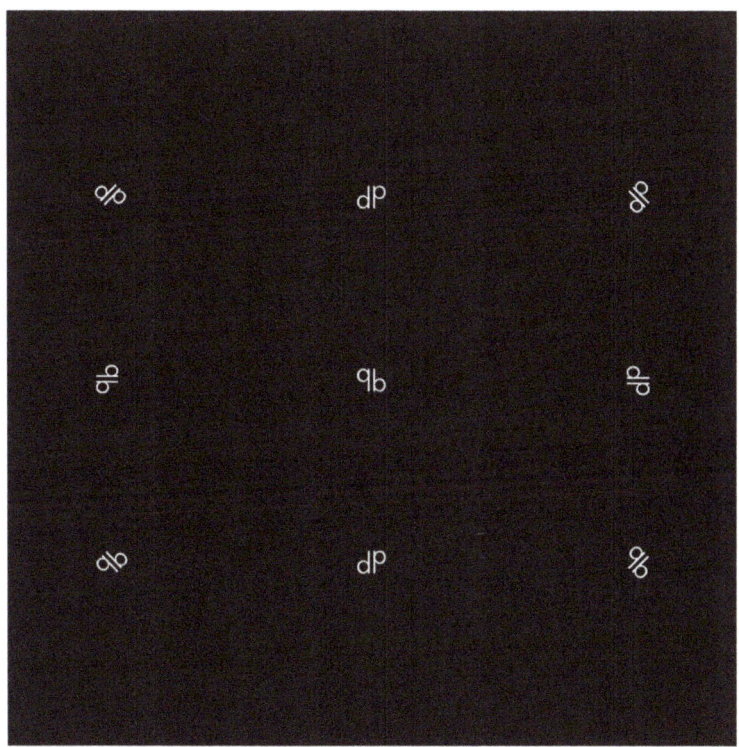

Let's try this out: what is authenticity exactly
Authentic solely means being genuine to oneself.
#realmoves #thelaydab

laydabshoe

Leather, as a byproduct of the food industry, is highly responsible and durable when handled right. The Sacchetto technique is a handmade process that involves more than 200 steps and denotes a specific style based on the principle of Native American moccasins. The soft leather encloses the shape of the foot on a light yet firm sole, breathable and with contact plate—the inner lining is sewn almost seamlessly to the upper leather like a small sack (sacchetto in Italian).
#bsuedeshoes #thelaydab

laydabshoe

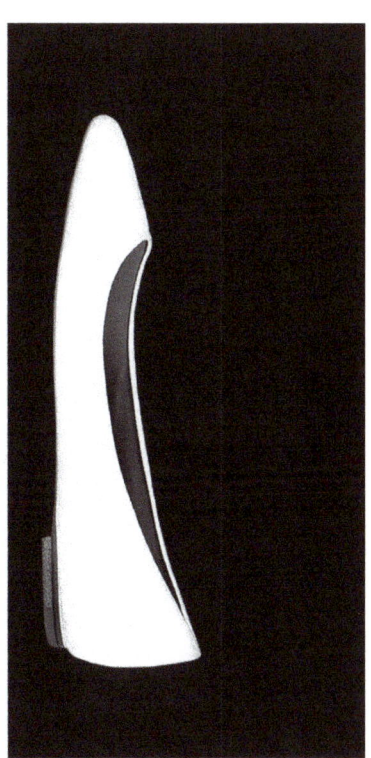

laydabshoe

Authenticity advanced, a shot in the dark
Being authentic is inherently connected to kindness and cannot
be maintained otherwise.
#blackakintoblue #thelaydab

laydabshoe

laydabshoe

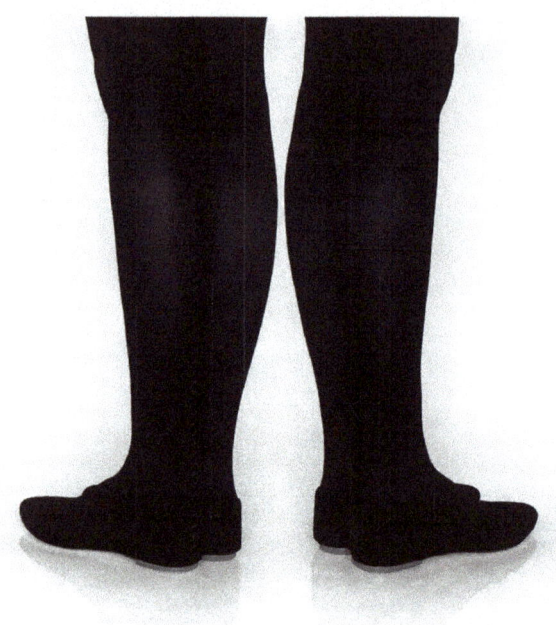

Lookin back / Movin on
blue note trip
#bridging #thelaydab

laydabshoe

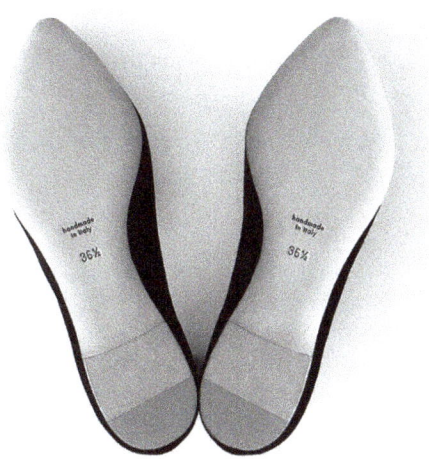

Finned
#travelshoe #thelaydab

laydabshoe

LAYDA b

36

Prepared for takeoff
#poise #thelaydab

laydabshoe

Archetype
#aesthetician #thelaydab

laydabshoe

In a way I'm a bit of a misfit, I suppose. Sade
#simplegrace #thelaydab

*The woman who follows the crowd
will usually go no further
than the crowd.
The woman who walks alone
is likely to find herself in places
no one has ever been before.*

A. Einstein

#trajectory #thelaydab

laydabshoe

Go Go Go Go! W. Clement Stone
photo Jonathan Livingston Seagull
#gopower #thelaydab

laydabshoe

New West
#positioned #thelaydab

When the sense is not that the glass is a half full
or half empty, the glass could also be fuller.
#idealist #thelaydab

laydabshoe

Flip the Script
#bluely #thelaydab

laydabshoe

Haiku Shell
An own universe, it's in a nutshell #superb
Whatever you stance
#hashtagshaiku #thelaydab

laydabshoe

laydabshoe

In this moment of suspended time, when the night is yet to find its star. A moment of perfection, a total moment. I am unable to express my confusion, my emotion, only this perfume is worthy of it. Jacques Guerlain #bluehour #thelaydab

laydabshoe

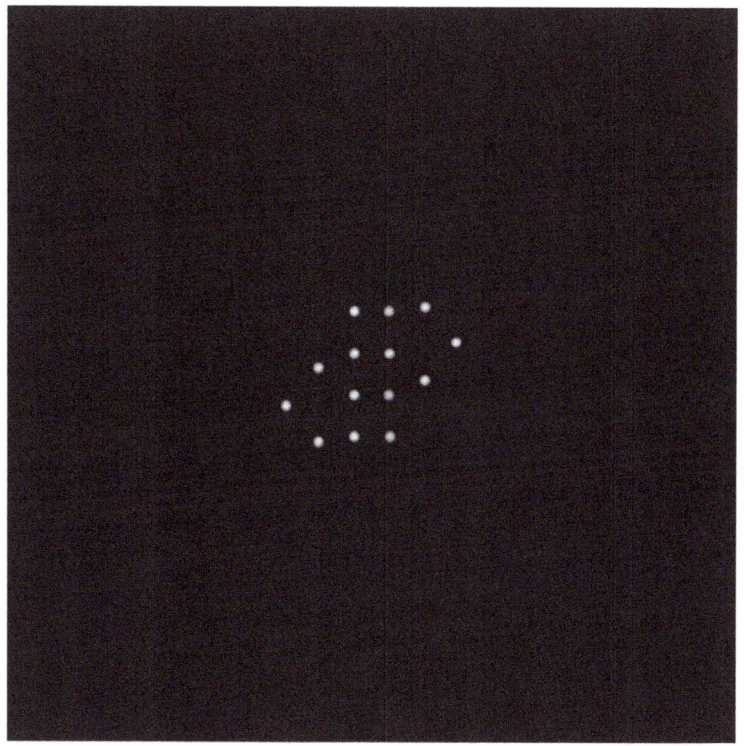

laydabshoe

Crescent
#traditionalknowkledge #thelaydab

The Layda b Giraffe
blackn'darkblue
#refinement #thelaydab

laydabshoe

Peace
#perfectstateofmind #thelaydab

For those who master the art of stillness, everything is possible.
#subtle #thelaydab

laydabshoe

The true aesthetician is also virtuous. from Quo Vadis
Season's greetings all!
#classisawayofbeing #thelaydab

laydabshoe

laydabshoe

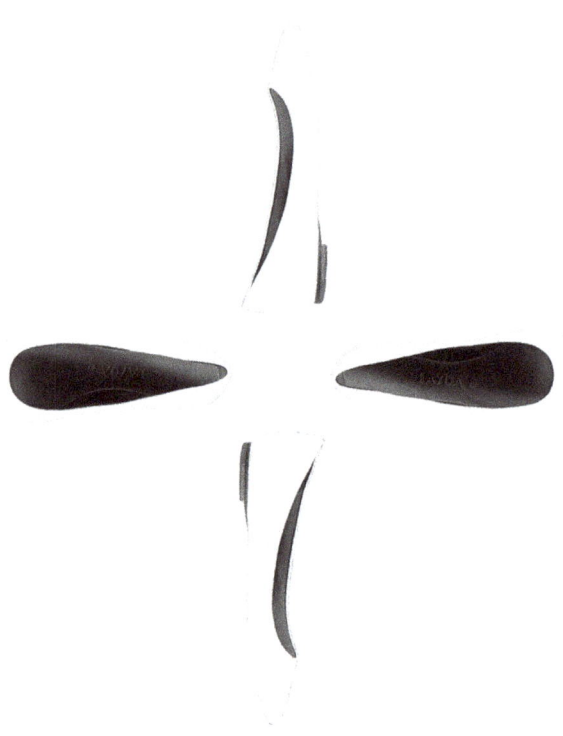

The 4 stoic virtues
wisdom, courage, moderation, justice
#artofstyle #thelaydab

laydabshoe

It is resolved by moving.
#doingisbeing #thelaydab

laydabshoe

Both ways work: values drive consciousness,
and consciousness drives values
#maninthemirror #thelaydab

*Anyone who knows Easter
cannot despair.*

Dietrich Bonhoeffer

Life and existence aren't the same pair
#ofshoes #thelaydab

laydabshoe

You must train your intuition—you must trust the small voice inside you which tells you exactly what to say, what to decide. Ingrid Bergman #nomoonnosun #thelaydab

laydabshoe

No moon no sun
#archetype #thelaydab

laydabshoe

Behold, the moon has risen,
The golden stars, they glisten
upon the heavens bright.
The forests rest in shadows,
and from the quiet meadows
white hazes rise into the night.
The world in stillness clouded
and soft in twilight shrouded,
so peaceful and so fair.
from the poem Evening Song
#culturalheritage #thelaydab

laydabshoe

laydabshoe

Haiku Bright fish
Two whales passing by, a stream with bright fish #cocoon
Walks any waters
#hashtaghaiku #thelaydab

laydabshoe

laydabshoe

Your excellence is flawless
#authenticist #thelaydab

The collection seeks to address the underlying causes of present imbalances. Looking ahead into the current societal situation, everyone, and especially women, is the target. Over and above is the linked desire for ongoing improvement for each of us.

be Aesthetician

laydabshoe

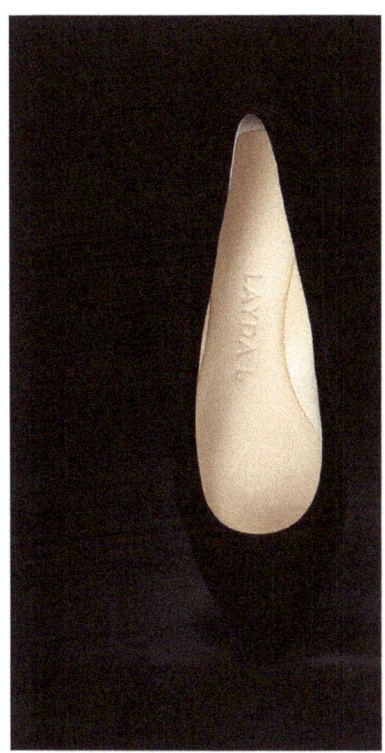 

Aesthetics and ease #thelaydab